HOW TO DRAW
SCIENCE FICTION

Mark Bergin

PowerKiDS
press™

New York

Published in 2012 by The Rosen Publishing Group, Inc.
29 East 21st Street, New York, NY 10010

Editor: Rob Walker
U.S. Editor: Kara Murray

Library of Congress Cataloging-in-Publication Data

Bergin, Mark.
How to draw science fiction / by Mark Bergin. — 1st ed.
        p. cm. — (How to draw)
Includes index.
ISBN 978-1-4488-4516-3 (library binding) — ISBN 978-1-4488-4527-9 (pbk.) —
ISBN 978-1-4488-4528-6 (6-pack)
1. Science fiction—Illustrations—Juvenile literature. 2. Drawing—Technique—Juvenile literature.
I. Title.
NC825.O9.B47 2012
741.2—dc22

2010053138

Manufactured in Heshan, China

CPSIA Compliance Information: Batch #SS1102PK: For Further Information contact
Rosen Publishing, New York, New York at 1-800-237-9932

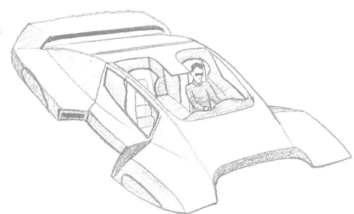

Contents

Making a Start

Learning to draw is about looking and seeing. Keep practicing and get to know your subject. Use a sketchbook to make quick drawings. Start by doodling, and experiment with shapes and patterns. There are many ways to draw. This book shows only some methods. Visit art galleries, look at artists' drawings, see how friends draw, but above all, find your own way.

Remember that practice makes perfect. If it looks wrong, start again. Keep working. The more you draw, the more you will learn.

Materials

Try using different types of drawing paper and materials. Experiment with charcoal, wax crayons, and pastels. All pens, from felt-tips to ballpoints, will make interesting marks. You could also try drawing with pen and ink on wet paper.

Silhouette is a style of drawing that mainly uses solid black shapes.

Ink silhouette

Ink

Lines drawn in **ink** cannot be erased, so keep your ink drawings sketchy and less rigid. Don't worry about mistakes as these lines can be lost in the drawing as it develops.

Adding light and shade to a drawing with an ink pen can be tricky. Use solid ink for the very darkest areas and cross-hatching (straight lines criss-crossing each other) for ordinary dark tones. Use hatching (straight lines running parallel to each other) for midrange tones and keep the lightest areas empty.

Hard pencils are grayer and soft pencils are blacker. Hard pencils are graded from #4 (the hardest) through #3 and #2½.

A **soft pencil** is a #1 pencil. A #2 pencil is right in the middle.

Wax crayons can be scraped away from parts of a drawing to create special effects.

Charcoal is very soft and can be used for big, bold drawings.

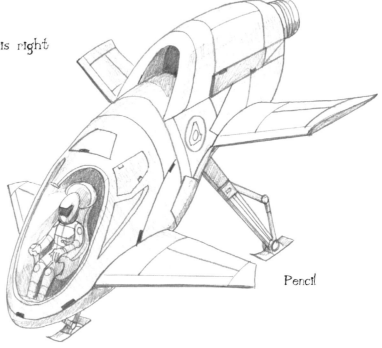

Pencil

Felt—tip

Pastels are softer than charcoal and come in a wide range of colors. Ask an adult to spray your pastel drawing with fixative to prevent it from smudging.

Felt—tips come in a range of line widths. The wider pens are good for filling in large areas of flat tone.

7

Perspective

If you look at any object from different viewpoints, you will see that the part that is closest to you looks larger, and the part farthest away from you looks smaller. Drawing in perspective is a way of creating a feeling of depth, of showing three dimensions on a flat surface.

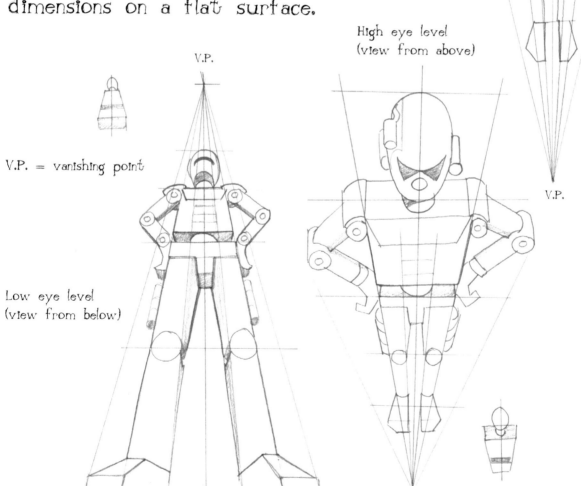

High eye level (view from above)

V.P.

V.P. = vanishing point

Low eye level (view from below)

V.P.

V.P.

Two-point perspective uses two vanishing points: one for lines running along the length of the object, and one on the opposite side for lines running across the width of the object.

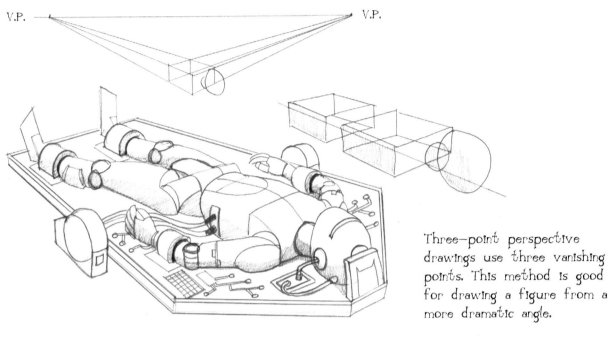

Three-point perspective drawings use three vanishing points. This method is good for drawing a figure from a more dramatic angle.

It may help you with perspective if you imagine that your figure fits into a rectangular block like this.

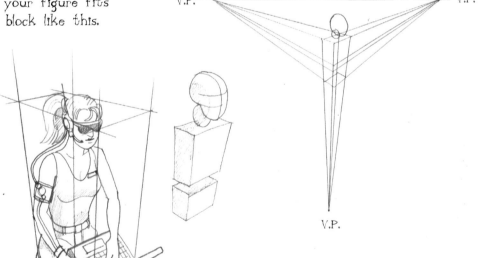

The vanishing point (V.P.) is the place in a perspective drawing where parallel lines appear to meet. The position of the vanishing point depends on the viewer's eye level. Sometimes a low viewpoint can give your drawing added drama.

9

Places and Planets

Be imaginative when drawing places in space. Try to make the landscapes and settings as exciting or unusual as possible.

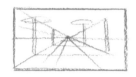

Roughly sketch construction lines for your drawings to help you.

Experiment by changing the eye level and vanishing points of your drawings (see page 8) to create a sense of drama.

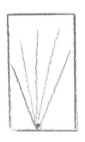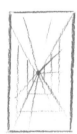

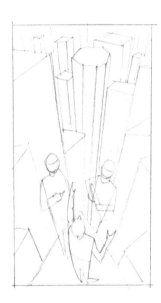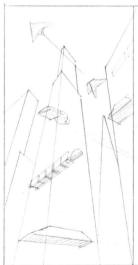

Once you have the basic shape of the drawing, you can start to add windows and other final details.

Use hatching to create
the texture of rock.

Draw stars and planets in the sky.

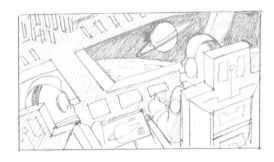

Try to draw something
interesting in both the
foreground and background.

To make your drawing look three-dimensional,
decide which side the light is coming from
so you can put in areas of shadow.

Spacecraft

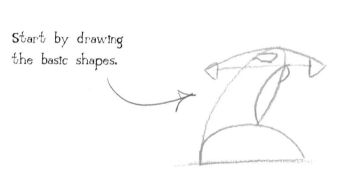

Space travelers use all sorts of unusual flying machines to move around space. Just like cars and planes today, they come in many different shapes and sizes.

Add a space traveler inside the cockpit of the spacecraft.

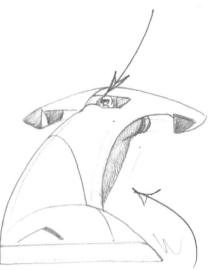

Start by drawing the basic shapes.

Draw two oval shapes joined together by a smaller rectangle.

Shade areas to make it appear three-dimensional.

Add bold, sweeping curves to the shapes to make it look futuristic.

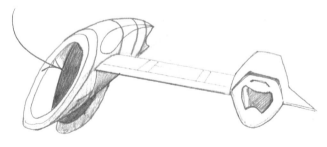

Use perspective (see pages 8—9) to make the craft look as though it is hurtling through space.

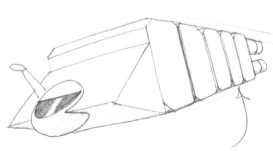

Round off the corners of the shapes.

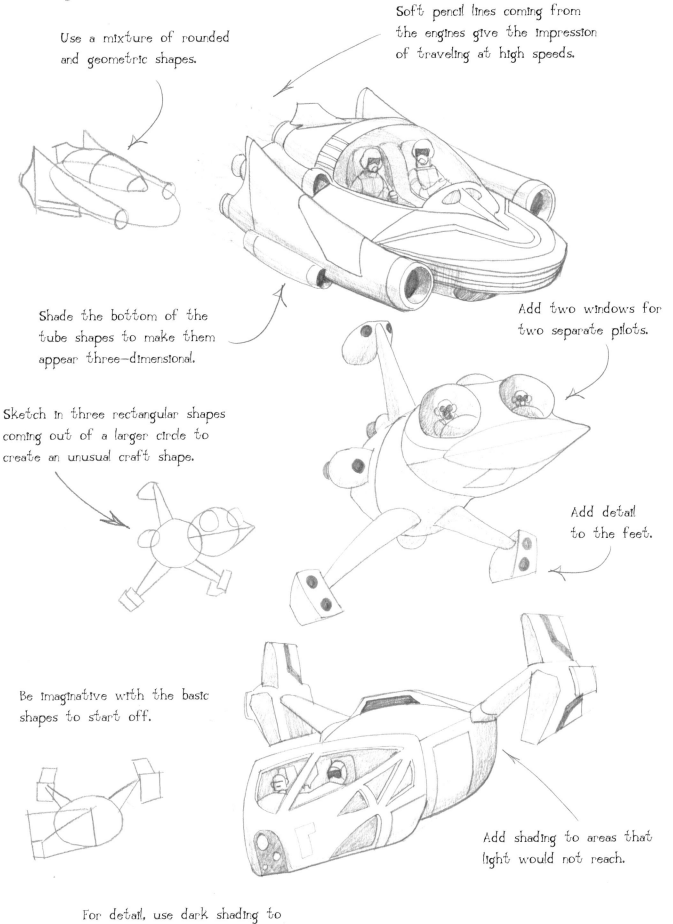

Use a mixture of rounded and geometric shapes.

Soft pencil lines coming from the engines give the impression of traveling at high speeds.

Shade the bottom of the tube shapes to make them appear three-dimensional.

Add two windows for two separate pilots.

Sketch in three rectangular shapes coming out of a larger circle to create an unusual craft shape.

Add detail to the feet.

Be imaginative with the basic shapes to start off.

Add shading to areas that light would not reach.

For detail, use dark shading to indicate any areas that go inward.

Vehicles

People in space drive various types of vehicles to jet between planets and travel around the galaxy. Some are designed for speed, some for comfort, and some even for combat.

For this space scooter, start by sketching a large oval shape with a triangle at the front.

Add curved lines and rounded shapes for the detail of the vehicle.

Draw an oval for the head, with helmet detail.

Add tube shapes for the limbs.

Shade the front of the vehicle to look like glass.

Sketch trianglular shapes on the front of the machine.

Draw circles for the joints.

Complete the detail of the driver by shading in the helmet and making his suit look futuristic.

Shade in the areas where light would not reach.

Remove any unwanted construction lines.

14

For the space car, start by sketching a large oval shape with a curved line through it where the side of the car meets the top.

Draw basic rounded shapes on the front.

Add a spoiler to the rear of the vehicle.

Make the shape at the front three-dimensional.

Sketch in the outline of the window.

Add curved lines.

Inside the cockpit, add the outline of two chairs and, using basic shapes, a pilot.

Shade the underside of the spoiler.

Shade in the driver and add hair and glasses.

Use soft shading to add detail to the inside of the cockpit.

Add shade to the underside of the vehicle.

Complete the vehicle by shading in the areas where light would not reach.

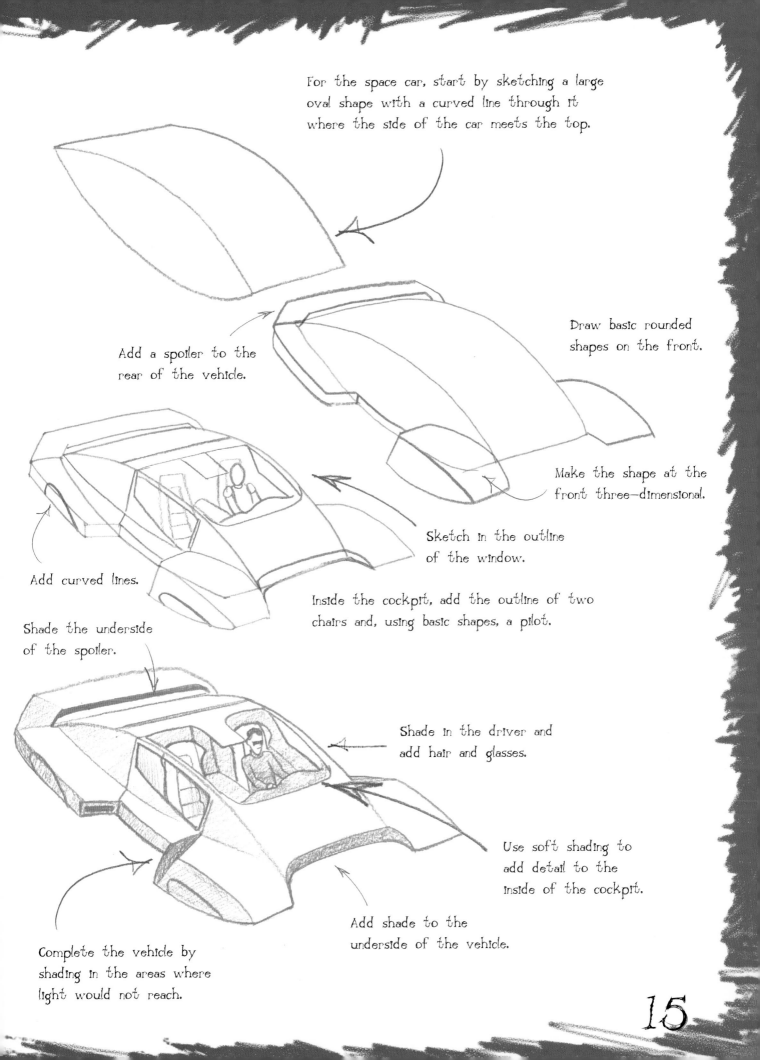

15

Space Stations

Space stations allow humans to live in outer space for a period of time, mainly to carry out scientific research and experiments. Be as creative as you like with your design.

Start by drawing basic shapes. Make some parts rounded and some geometric.

Add shading to the shapes to make them look three-dimensional.

Notice how the design is built up from larger and smaller versions of the same basic shape.

Be imaginative with the shape of the space station.

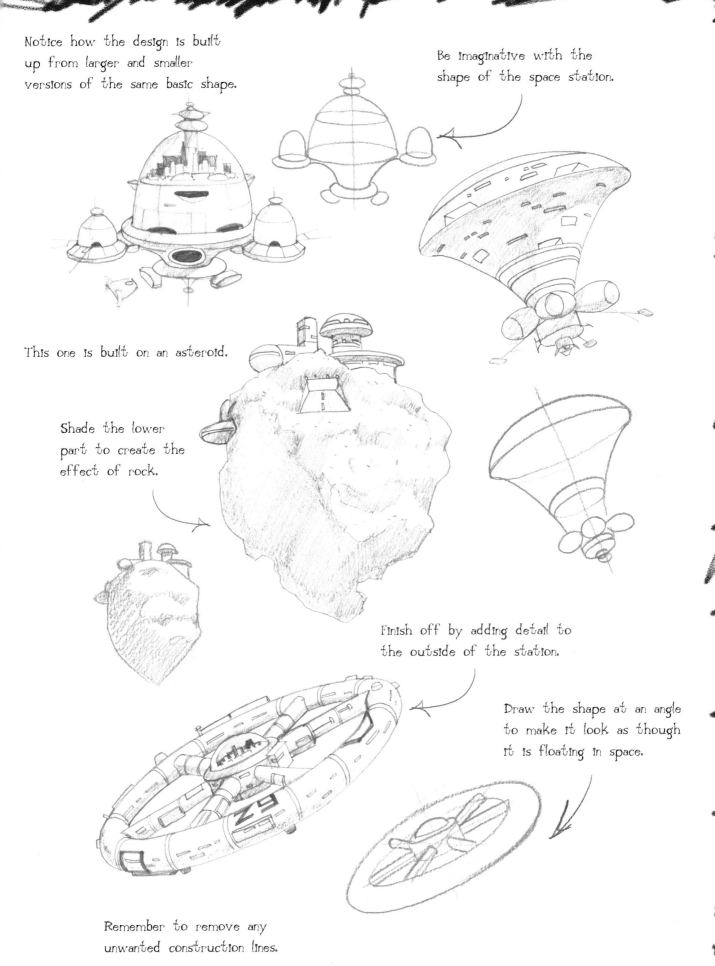

This one is built on an asteroid.

Shade the lower part to create the effect of rock.

Finish off by adding detail to the outside of the station.

Draw the shape at an angle to make it look as though it is floating in space.

Remember to remove any unwanted construction lines.

17

Human Characters

Drawing a human science—fiction character can be broken down into easy stages. Follow the steps shown here to create your own astronauts and space explorers.

Start by sketching these simple shapes.

Draw circles and ovals for the head, main body, and hips.

Add hair.

Use straight guidelines and a vertical center line to experiment with the proportions of the body.

Draw straight lines for the limbs and circles for the joints.

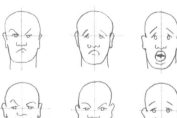

Then, start to build up the basic shapes and features of the figure.

Change the stance of the figure by moving the straight lines of the limbs.

Turn the lines of the arms and legs into simple tube shapes.

Use construction lines to position the features of the face.

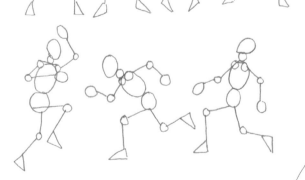

Do not be afraid to exaggerate the features for comic effect.

Helmets must be worn when traveling in space.

Leave a vertical stripe of white when shading the visors. This is the light reflecting off the tinted glass.

Think about how the helmet would look in profile.

Add detail to the surface of the clothing to make it look as futuristic as possible.

Complete the detail of the faces.

Experiment with different facial expressions and body poses.

Sketch a circle and inner rings on the shoulders.

Draw a belt with pouches for tools.

Add a stripe detail to the helmets.

Shade in a suggestion of rocky ground.

Shade the areas where light would not reach.

Draw futuristic boots.

Robots and Droids

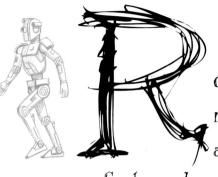

Robots are electronic machines that are often found in science-fiction books and films. Androids are made to look and act like humans and can be very intelligent.

This detail looks a little like a circuit board. Add some to your drawing to make it look more robotic.

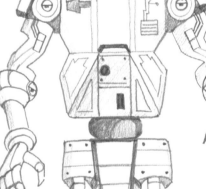

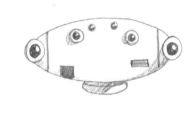

Try to make faces from unusual shapes. Use buttons, dials, and switches.

Small circles can look like bolts that are holding the robot together.

Add dots and lines to the robot's metalwork to add interest.

Shade some areas where the light would not reach.

Robots' hands can have fingers or be more mechanical.

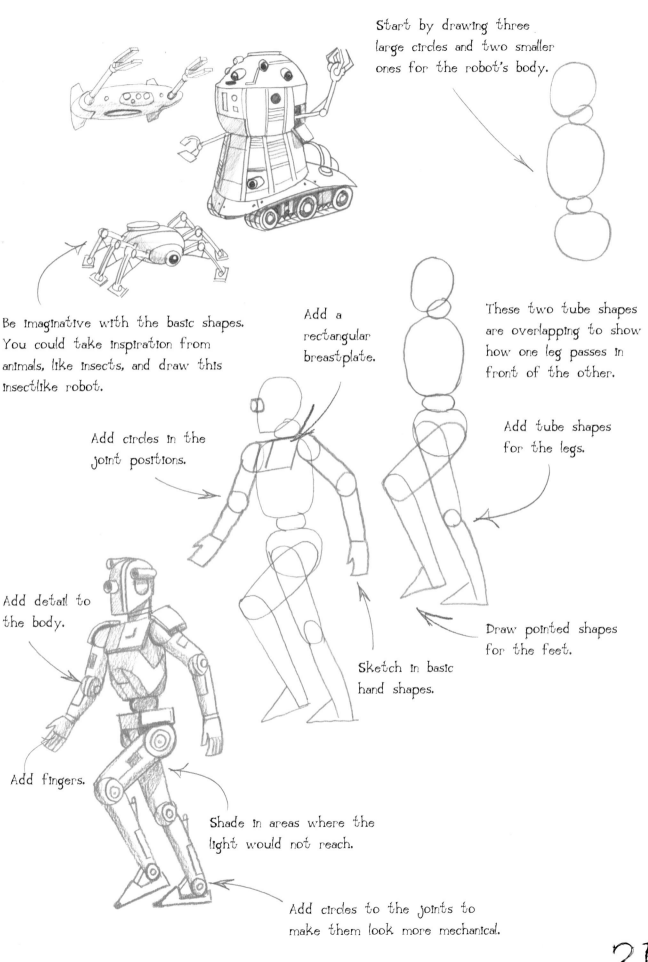

Start by drawing three large circles and two smaller ones for the robot's body.

Be imaginative with the basic shapes. You could take inspiration from animals, like insects, and draw this insectlike robot.

Add a rectangular breastplate.

These two tube shapes are overlapping to show how one leg passes in front of the other.

Add circles in the joint positions.

Add tube shapes for the legs.

Add detail to the body.

Draw pointed shapes for the feet.

Sketch in basic hand shapes.

Add fingers.

Shade in areas where the light would not reach.

Add circles to the joints to make them look more mechanical.

21

Space Machinery

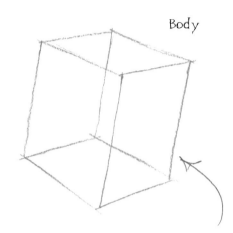

Space machines are used for exploring new planets. Their powerful legs can keep them steady when traveling over dangerous terrain. The driver controls the machine from the inside.

Body

Draw a three-dimensional box for the main body of the space machine.

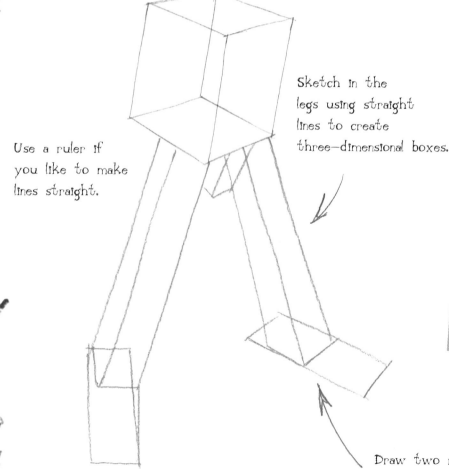

Sketch in the legs using straight lines to create three-dimensional boxes.

Use a ruler if you like to make lines straight.

Draw two rectangles to form the base of the feet.

Using a Mirror

Hold your picture up to a mirror so you can look at it in reverse. This will help you see mistakes.

Add rectangles to the shoulders.

Using straight lines and circles, sketch in the shape of the arms.

Draw basic rectangular shapes for the window on the front of the machine.

Add the knee joints by drawing two circles and some straight lines.

Add a driver inside the cockpit of the space machine.

Complete the elbow, making the joint look mechanical.

Add fingers.

Add detail to the machine. Straight lines on its surface show how it is mechanically made.

Decide where the light is coming from, then shade the areas where it would not reach.

Add shading to create craters and a rocky terrain.

23

Alien Characters

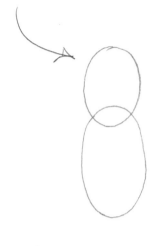

In science fiction, aliens are creatures that do not come from planet Earth. No one knows what they really look like, so use your imagination to create your own crazy space alien.

Draw two ovals slightly overlapping.

Add snakelike shapes for tentacles.

Draw two parallel lines for the base of the top oval.

Draw some eyes on stalks and shade the oval to look like glass.

Sketch in branchlike shapes for the arms.

Add detail to the body.

Shade the areas where light would not reach.

Add a scaly pattern to the tentacles.

Draw unusually shaped heads to
create bizarre alien forms.

Some aliens have more
than two eyes.

Add ferocious,
sharp teeth.

You could take inspiration from
the features of dinosaurs.

Add darker areas of shading to
the drawing for dramatic effect.

Add wing shapes.

Science-fiction aliens come in all
different shapes and sizes.

Stretch out arms and legs to
make spidery alien body shapes.

25

Cartoon Aliens

There are no rules when drawing aliens. Add extra eyes and legs, draw hands with three fingers, or make the neck very long and skinny. Perhaps even add a flying saucer!

To make this one-eyed alien, start by drawing two ovals joined by a long tube shape.

Add two rounded shapes for feet.

Draw curved lines for arm shapes.

Add shading to the areas where light would not reach.

Draw markings on the alien's body.

Add one large eye and shading.

Add details to the feet.

Sketch in the toes.

Here is a cute alien with his own flying saucer.

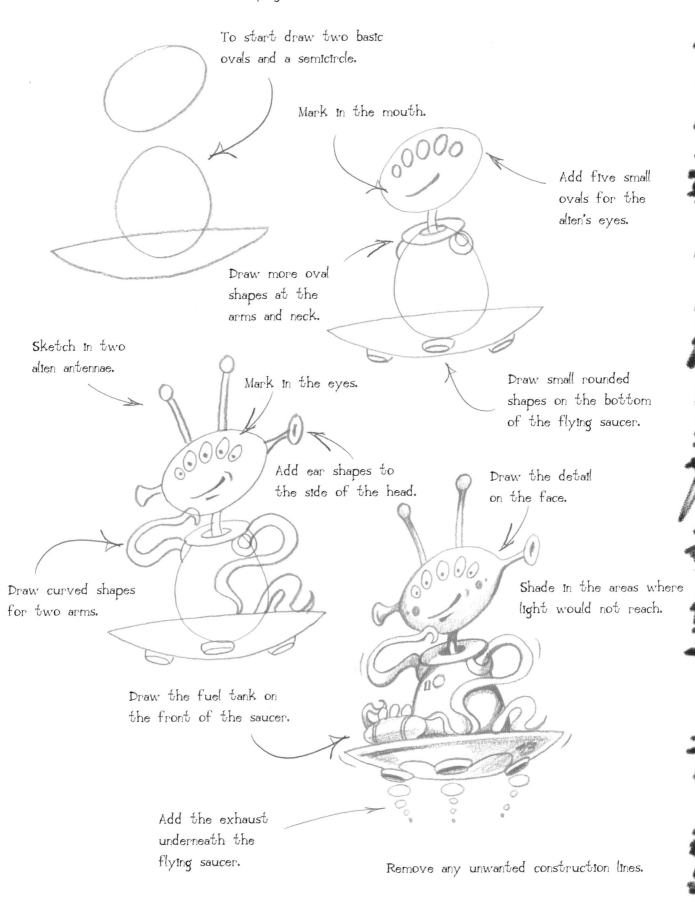

To start draw two basic ovals and a semicircle.

Mark in the mouth.

Add five small ovals for the alien's eyes.

Draw more oval shapes at the arms and neck.

Sketch in two alien antennae.

Mark in the eyes.

Draw small rounded shapes on the bottom of the flying saucer.

Add ear shapes to the side of the head.

Draw the detail on the face.

Draw curved shapes for two arms.

Shade in the areas where light would not reach.

Draw the fuel tank on the front of the saucer.

Add the exhaust underneath the flying saucer.

Remove any unwanted construction lines.

Spaceman and Robots

This spaceman loves to explore new planets, especially when he stumbles across new and interesting alien robots!

Draw two large circles slightly overlapping.

Draw a visor shape on the helmet.

Sketch in two curved arm shapes.

Shade in the visor, leaving a spot white for a highlight.

Add detail to the face of the spaceman.

Draw curved leg shapes.

Draw fingers.

Add basic rounded shapes for the feet.

Add shading and detail to the space suit.

Indicate the shape of an oxygen pack.

Draw vertical lines on the base of the space boots.

Start by drawing basic rounded shapes for the outlines of the two robots.

You can use different-sized shapes to create different characters.

Add circles to mark the positions of the arms.

Add an antenna.

Add rounded shapes with circle knee joints.

Draw eyes and a mouth.

Shade the robots to look like shiny metal.

Draw rounded foot shapes.

Add branch shapes for arms.

Add the arms using straight lines and circular shapes.

Shade the areas where light would not reach.

29

Cartoon Scene

To make your space-character drawings even more exciting, you can place the aliens and astronauts in a scene. This can give your drawing added drama and a sense of action. This example shows the characters meeting on an alien planet, but you can use your imagination to draw them in any situation you like.

First draw a box with a horizon line running through it, then draw the construction lines of the characters themselves. Any vanishing points (see pages 8—9) should be on the horizon line.

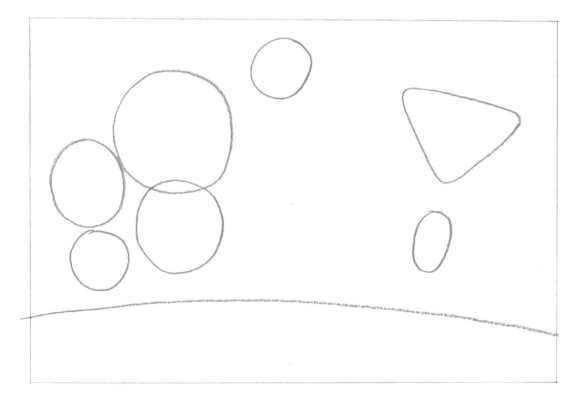

Draw simple shapes for
planets in the background.

Sketch in the basic shapes of the spaceman and
aliens and mark the positions of their features.

Once you have the basic shape of the drawing,
you can start to add detail. Add stars in the
sky and craters on the ground.

Draw the final details of
the space characters.

Glossary

construction lines (kun-STRUK-shun LYNZ) Guidelines used in the early stages of a drawing. They are usually erased later.

fixative (FIK-suh-tiv) A type of resin that is sprayed over a finished drawing to prevent smudging. It should be used only by an adult.

galleries (GA-luh-reez) Rooms or buildings that show works of art.

perspective (per-SPEK-tiv) A method of drawing in which near objects are shown larger than faraway objects to give an impression of depth.

pose (POHZ) The position assumed by a figure.

proportion (pruh-POR-shun) The correct relationship of scale between each part of the drawing.

silhouette (sih-luh-WET) A drawing that shows only a flat dark shape, like a shadow.

sketchbook (SKECH-buhk) A book in which quick drawings are made.

vanishing point (VA-nish-ing POYNT) The place in a perspective drawing where parallel lines appear to meet.

Index

Web Sites

Due to the changing nature of Internet links, PowerKids Press has developed an online list of Web sites related to the subject of this book. This site is updated regularly. Please use this link to access the list:

www.powerkidslinks.com/htd/scifi/